IN SEARCH OF EROS

ELIZABETH BREWSTER

IN SEARCH OF
EROS

CLARKE, IRWIN & COMPANY LIMITED
TORONTO, VANCOUVER

Some of the poems in this book have been
published in *Far Point, Fiddlehead, Inscape,
Malahat Review, New: American and Canadian
Poetry, Poetry (Chicago), Quarry, Canadian
Forum, Canadian Author and Bookman, Queen's
Quarterly, Saturday Night.*

Four of the poems appear in *Mountain Moving
Day: Poems by Women,* Elaine Gill, editor,
The Crossing Press, New York.

A number of these poems were writtten while
the poet held a Senior Arts Award from the
Canada Council.

ISBN 0-7720-0715-2

1 2 3 4 5 6   BP   79 78 77 76 75 74

Published simultaneously in the United States by
Books Canada Inc., 33 East Tupper Street,
Buffalo, N.Y. 14203 and in the United Kingdom
by Books Canada Limited, 17 Cockspur Street,
Suite 600, London SW1Y 5BP

Printed in Canada

To some friends
(in place of dedication)

In the old days how we all talked together
of building a new language, every word
fresh-minted, untouched by the elders. Poetry,
some argued, should be pure and meaningless,
with words like colours on an abstract canvas,
making a pattern pleasing but remote.
Others thought poems should be like the posters
we saw in war time, vigorous and swift,
carrying their message plain upon their front,
"Do this, do that, vote in the prescribed way,
be wary or the Enemy will get you."
Some thought that poems should be strange and subtle,
with seven or seventy ambiguities,
image piled upon image to express
meanings dream-deep and devious. Some preferred
words clear and hard as icicles or mirrors,
reflecting—what?

Now some who were most eager in dispute
no longer strive; and I, who was perhaps
less of your company than the others were,
being given to writing casually and as I pleased,
can find no theory how or what to write,
merely reflect my small and personal world,
a second-hand vision or a passing love,
yet must maintain, though intermittently,
the worth of the argument, my deep concern.

CONTENTS

I THE MAGIC ROD

For P.K.P. / 3
Speak to me / 5
Consulting the I Ching / 7
The magic rod / 9
Poems for an audience of one / 10
Poems for your hands / 11
Slow motion / 14
Tongue-tied / 14
Time machine / 15
Gifts / 16
Chill / 16
On impermanence / 17
Nursery rhyme / 18
Empty-handed / 18
When sea birds cry / 18
Greeting / 19
Year's end / 19
Summer evening lightning / 20

II IN SEARCH OF EROS

The prince who married the sleeping beauty / 23
The princess addresses the frog prince / 25
The boy who married the frog princess / 26
Cinderella / 28
Princess of Egypt / 29
The giant's heart / 30
Kind and unkind / 31
Sister selves / 34
Stage setting / 34
Old Lear, the crazy king / 35
Fool's song / 35
Lear / 36
In search of Eros / 37
Psyche and Cupid / 42
Rosa / 42
Willie Lump Lump / 43
Portrait of a woman with pigeons / 44
Romance / 44
Three sonnets on The Scarlet Letter / 45

III INANNA

Death of the gods / 49
For the unknown goddess / 51
Moon / 52
Inanna / 52
Three joyful mysteries / 53
Man with gospel message (Verbal transcription) / 55
Jesus revolution hits Alberta / 57
The blue pen / 59
Playing Indian / 61
Trapped / 62

IV PILGRIM

On the nature of the hero / 65
My unkind self / 66
Marvel / 67
Mirrors / 68
Night air / 68
Pastoral tradition / 69
The seige of Troy / 70
The return of Homer / 71
Golden West / 72
Alden Nowlan in the Winnipeg air terminal / 73
Poem for Al Purdy / 74
Poem for a young sorceress / 75
39 North Castle Street, Edinburgh, 1820 / 76
At the poet's birthplace / 77
Return of the native / 78
View from window / 79
Immigrants / 79
The poet in the last days / 80
Earthquake / 81
Seasonal / 82
On the death by burning of Kimberly Hammer,
    May 1972 / 83
Judgment / 84
Waiting room / 85
Lost / 85
Wilderness dream / 86
Disqualification / 87
Pilgrim / 88

I
THE MAGIC ROD

3 *For P.K.P.*

I

Do you think
there are interconnections
rhymes rhythms recurrences
that people form a pattern

Do you think there are echoes
that whispers reverberate

Do you think destiny holds us
like wool in her fingers
weaving us in and out?

When we are as far as
sea from prairie
the weaving fingers
tighten the wool.

II

Child on the seashore
digging moist sand
into a bucket
playing with pebbles
playing with water
feels all the tides
of all the oceans
rise in her veins
is herself
is I
is you
is everyone
is nobody.

III

In a grain of sand
in a snowflake
there are patterns.
A dreamer drew
the Holy Ghost in the form of a spiral,
and the Milky Way
is also a spiral.

IV

In and out
in and out
we move as in a dance
an elaborate ballet
though I am clumsy
spoil the pattern

except in dreams, where I move
as you move
perfectly
your double
the perfect ballerina

V

And the others move
swans, witches, the prince,
choric observers,
we all move
nobody first
all equal
reflecting one another

moved by the tide
the dance
the snowstorm
the expanding spiral

5   *Speak to me*

Love, speak to me
in the language of birds
their incoherent cries

speak to me
in the language of snakes
uncoiling silently

speak to me
in the language of soft furry animals

speak to me
in the language of fishes
swimming dark pools

Love, speak to me
in the language of men

I came before, oracle,
but only to the edge of the cave.
I was afraid to go in
and you were sleeping too deeply
for my voice to bring you out.

But now I am ready.
Now I will sink down
into that darkness,
drown if necessary in the wells
of your quicksand eyes.

Speak, sibyl, with your high
ancient voice,
the twittering
of dead swallows;

speak rhymes and riddles
and cracked wisdom;
tell me the world's fortune;
tell me my own fate;
tell me your most true,
most beautiful lies.

7 *Consulting the I Ching*

I

(Hexagram 48: Ching; Wells)

I am consulting the I Ching
with six pennies, four dimes,
and (since I am short of silver)
two Toronto subway tokens.

The hexagram I am guided to
is for Ching: Wells.

The well is muddy:
it has been forsaken
by men and birds.

Water seeps away from the well
and is wasted.
(The subject of this line of the hexagram
has no one to cooperate above him.)

The well has been cleared out,
but is not used.
"If the king were intelligent,
both he and we
might receive the benefit of it."

The lining of the well
has been skilfully laid.

The fifth line of the hexagram
(which is the most important)
shows a clear well
of sparkling water
from which the traveller drinks
and refreshes himself.

8   The sixth line shows
     the water brought to the top of the well,
     standing uncovered.
     This line suggests sincerity.

     "There will be great good fortune."

     II

     (Hexagram 46: Sheng; Advance)

     The subject of the hexagram
     advances upward
     with the welcome of those above him.

     The subject offers
     the vernal sacrifices.

     The subject ascends
     into an empty city.

     The subject is employed by the king
     to present his offerings.

     The subject makes no errors.
     He therefore enjoys good fortune.

     The subject advances upward
     blindly

     to the most dangerous place.

     III

     (Hexagram 54: Kuei Mei; Going Home)

     The hexagram denotes
     the marriage of the younger sister
     in the position of handmaid
     to the true wife.

     She delays
     she puts off the time
     but it will come.

9   The sleeves of the princess
    are not equal to those
    of her younger sister.

    The moon is almost full.

    By the marriage of a younger sister
    is suggested
    the relation between heaven and earth
    which is the source of fruitfulness.

    "Any action will be evil."
    "There will be good fortune."

The magic rod

The magic rod
divides the waters
opens a way through the waves.

The magic rod
planted in the ground
becomes a tree.

The magic rod
brings plagues
is awe-full
is fear
is death.

The magic rod
heals all hurt
is blossoming
fragrance
is life.

Why do you write?
someone has asked me.
Is it for fame or fortune?
Do you wish to communicate
to a larger audience?
Have you an important message?

I would like to say,
though I don't,
that I write for none of these reasons.

I am writing now
to pass the time
while I am waiting
for you to telephone.

I

Your hand, which has written these poems
that I read in the spring evening,
has also traced poems on my flesh.
The inside of my mouth
has flowered into lyrics;
my breasts are rhymed
couplets;
my belly is smoothed to a sonnet;
and the cave of my body
is a found poem.

II

You say you are an old man
un viellard
and I remember you middle-aged when I was young
yet I feel a wistful youthfulness in you
the unquenched spirit
still flaming in spite of time and wrinkles.

Desire is sad
across this gulf of time.

But touch me lightly
touch my tongue with yours.

Perhaps I could not have stood
the total blaze
of your youth and strength.

III

You disarrange my life.
I cannot predict you.
Saying that you do not know me,
I mean that I do not know you.
I know I could not live with you,
but am frightened also
that I may find it hard to live
without you.

I try to find out facts
about you, so as to feel safe with you.
I want to know all about your brothers
and what games you played as a child
and whether you were unhappy
and if you are afraid of anything.
All this I shall put together;
I shall make a file on you.

In return, I am willing to let you know
that I am afraid of bridges
and of strangers.

V

Without my glasses on
I cannot see you
am only aware of
arms, legs, a head,
the feel of skin
and hair.

You might be God
or my father
or someone I loved when I was young
who is now dead.

You might be a king
or an astronaut.

You might be an oak.

VI

"These are the sort of kisses
Catullus meant," you say.

I wonder if Lesbia ever
wrote any poems.
What a pity
no archaeologist has ever found them.

Let us not be
exclusively solemn.
In spite of the theory
that lust is a serious passion,
there is time even in bed
for a little light
verse.

VIII

"The body knows its mate,"
you say truly
and yet we have our minor difficulties.

But anyhow you tell me
"Next time I'll bring a sign saying
     We shall overcome."

IX

You telephone me from your office
where I feel you are bored.

I too have been bored
spring feverish
but I do not say so.

The inconvenience of joy
is that it is habit forming.

X

A pigeon walks along
my window sill
to prove that spring is here.

I do not need his proof
now that I am able to imagine
that we are both young again.

We make love in the afternoon
with the curtains closed.
Cars drive past the window.
A car door slams below us.
Someone is walking down the hotel corridor
knocking on doorways.
We hold our breath till whoever it is goes past.
Your hand rests motionless
on my bare shoulder.
I trace with one finger
the curve of your left eyebrow.

Tongue-tied

When we are both dressed
I feel shy with you.
In the restaurant
I look across the table at you
and admire
this distinguished stranger,
as I admire you sometimes
when I see you in a room full of people
talking to someone else.

I feel obliged to make small talk to you
and I forget all the questions
I wanted to ask
and the profound and beautiful things
I would say if I were not tongue-tied.

I am only comforted thinking
that some time again
we shall be naked together.

You tell me that doctors in
the Neurological Institute
can give a signal to the brain
and bring back lost time,
a whole day's sights, sounds, tastes, touches,
all its joys and tedium mixed
real as it was lived.

And I wonder if twenty years from now
I may want to bring back this day,
the hot moist afternoon,
the sound of traffic
outside the open window,
the feel of naked bodies
twined together,
the absurd bed creaking
beneath our weight

even the sense of sadness
when you leave too soon.

I know what you give me, but am not sure
what I give you. Is it just this
pleasure of touch and strangeness?
Are you aware
of my thoughts floating behind my eyes?

When you first touched me
it was the hopeless loves of my youth I thought of;
but now it is you yourself diving
into my depths, swimming
beside me, along my shores. Oh, love,
can I give you anything
so sweet and piercing as this pain?

Chill

Like all the women who sleep alone
in Chinese poems,
I shiver with the cold.

I would rather have you to warm me
than either a blanket or a poem,
but what can I do?
I pull both poem and blanket
over me now
but neither of them breathes.

Knowing that I cannot say
I will love you forever
or even perhaps for a very long time,
because time itself is against my loving,
and space,
and the sweep and tide of life,
and the restlessness of your will

(yes, and my will, which fears
the danger of love,
its power to hurt)

yet nevertheless I wish I could say it,
and wish to deny
that what is impermanent
is therefore of no importance.

A little longer
I hold your hands in my mind,
and some loneliness in you
which I could not touch,
and the wrong side of your face,
which you did not want me to see;

and I want so much to reach you
across time and space,
to lay my hand on yours,
that it almost seems I might,
and that I might love you,
after all, a little longer.

Nursery rhyme

My love was past noon
when I was young,
but his heart was light
and his arms were strong.

He was clever,
he was witty,
liked the girls
when they were pretty,

loved to make love,
and knew how too.
Without my love
what shall I do?

Empty-handed

What can we do for one another?
I see that you are afraid of age and death,
and I am afraid of life without tenderness.
Can I give you youth? Can you give me love?

What is there to do,
but hold each other's hands in pity
and sit on this dark shore waiting
for the tides to wash over us?

When sea birds cry

When sea birds cry above the prairie,
when salt winds wash the open plain,
when icebergs melt in the depths of winter
I'll dream I see my love again.

I'll dream your mouth is on my mouth, love;
I'll dream your hand upon my breast.
I'll dream the night is long as winter
when in your arms I find my rest.

19 *Greeting*

I walked this morning alone
through the bright white streets
past the white curve of the river.
It was Christmas morning.
Almost nobody was walking.
A man I did not know
called out to me, "Merry Christmas."
I saw his breath steaming
in the blue air.
Answering his words, I wondered
if you were maybe
thinking of me.

Year's end

Unbelievable this whiteness
new as spring blossoms,
all the trees covered with it
and fine drops of it falling
down from strung wire
and all the flat roof of
the newspaper office down below
bright with it.
Airy and white
trees cluster around spires;
smokestacks breathe white,
white clouds float
in the pale sky.

How suddenly this city
which seemed ugly
rises dazzling
as a once-plain woman glowing
beautifully
in the naked eye of the
long-awaited lover.

At one time I would have drawn the curtains
to keep out this lightning storm,
but I remember you said
that you liked lightning
and wanted, when you died, to be struck by a
     thunderbolt—
so godlike a way of being transported.

So I watch the eerie sky,
its blackness
lit by the sudden gleam, the sharp daggers.
I see the church tower upright against the glare,
a stage castle in the midst of shellfire.
A double flame, like a pair of compasses,
squeezes itself shut above the tower.

You walk in my mind,
a winged superman,
somewhere above the tower,
your feet scattering sparks,
your hair in flames,
arrows of thunder
quivering in your hand.

II
IN SEARCH OF EROS

I thought I had accomplished an adventure
to have chopped my way through the trees
that had grown up
around the sleeping palace,
to have pushed through the stiff,
almost unyielding door
into the passageway.

It was a country summer palace
like an overgrown farmhouse,
Victorian as carved fruit,
full of bric-a-brac and dozing parrots.
In the dusty afternoon
her father snoozed in his stuffed chair,
his beard still growing;
her mother's knitting
fell over the folds of her black bombazine
full-skirted afternoon gown.
They must have expected callers.

Upstairs, the princess
lay on her bed, as pink and beautiful
as previously reported.
She had been reading
a novel from the circulating library,
full of Lady Gertrude and Sir Hugh
and a poet and a governess
and a chimney sweep who was a long-lost heir.
The book was still open at page two hundred.

24   I awakened her
     to a thoroughly satisfactory surprise.
     She thought I was Sir Hugh
     or perhaps the poet.
     Later we became better acquainted.

     For a few months after the wedding
     we were happy.
     Now I am not so sure.
     She is still beautiful,
     but I find she thinks my parents
     are full of crazy modern ideas,
     and sometimes she seems happier
     talking to my grandfather
     than when she is with me.

     I've never been able to get her to give up
     those whalebone corsets she still fancies.

The princess addresses the frog prince

Oh, Frog Prince, Frog Prince,
it was not for you
that I dropped my golden ball
down into the deep water.

It was only by chance
that I dropped it at all.
I intended to stand still
holding the ball safe in my hand
and to look at myself reflected
with my gold crown on my hair
in the pond's surface.

Never in all the stories
was there a more beautiful princess.

And when the ball slipped
and fell from my hand
among the water lilies,
if I expected anyone to rise
from beneath the water

it was a merman or a drowned prince
who would be brought to life
by my eyes.

Never mind, you have a fine voice.
I will take you out of the water
to play in my garden.
I will even take you into the palace.
You shall sit by my gold plate
at dinner time
and be my ugly pet
and sing me songs.

My eldest brother shot an arrow
into the heart of the town.
The girl who picked it up
was a fine lady.
My second brother shot an arrow
over the land.
The girl who picked it up
was a farmer's daughter.

One wife wore a gold gown
and smelled of musk.
One wife wore homespun
and smelled of hay and apples.

I too shot an arrow,
but I was the family fool,
and only a frog in the pond
swam to me with my arrow.
"Woe's me," I said,
"for I must marry a frog,
and how my brothers will laugh
when they come to visit me."

My two brothers' wives
wove cloth for their wedding sheets.
The farm girl wove coarse canvas.
The lady wove a cobweb
too frail to last,
but my frog wife wove sheets
strong as reed grass,
delicate as dragonfly wings,
to wrap us snug.

27   My two brothers' wives
baked bread on baking day.
One baked it sour,
the other heavy.
But oh, my little frog wife,
she baked a loaf as light
as a water lily petal,
and honey sweet.

And my brothers' wives said,
"Let us have a great party.
The one of us who dances best
Shall be queen of us all."
The lady could dance a minuet,
the farm girl could square-dance,
but how could my poor little frog wife dance?

My eldest brother's wife
wore star-shaped earrings;
my second brother's wife
wore daisies in her hair.
But my own little wife
wore scarves of lake water.
She danced like ripples,
she danced like foam.

She was land and wave,
she was girl and mermaid.
When I kissed her mouth
she was queen of us all.

How many girls, washing the supper dishes,
have dreamed this dream:
the great ballroom lit with flaring torches;
velvet and satin crowds
and breasts of diamond,
the stylized ritual of the mating dance;
and underneath the jewelled candelabra
the prince entering
to leap higher than the other males
hold the heroine whirling
in the palm of one hand,
create her beauty
so that in the softened light
she glows a flame or flower.

Afterwards she runs through the garden
barefoot
her single slipper in her hand
her hair down her shoulders;
and, because she forgot time in the prince's arms,
must count time in the passage of long days.

But at length (in the fairy tale)
the prince comes to the door
holding the slipper
in his hand; and only the foot
of the girl washing dishes
will fit the shoe.
                    Prince and princess
dance through the wet garden
under the trees of summer,
and all the ice has gone out of the river.

The princess, walking by the shore,
found the abandoned child
nested in grasses like a bird.
She clapped her hands and smiled.

Her fans, her slaves, her peacock plumes,
her dark Egyptian face
hovered above the baby's head.
She took him to her breast.

Her plaything and her almost son,
he grew up strong and tall.
She gave him jewels for his ears
and a toy golden ball.

Almost Egyptian, almost prince,
he danced, he rode, he sang.
The golden princess smiled to see
that he was growing man.

Lady, when Moses was full-grown
did he abandon you?
Or did you die before that time?
I hope you did not know

what troubles from your kindness came.
I hope that you died young
and had no other first-born
than this one that you found.

Find where the giant's heart is.
Then you will have
power over his life.

He has planted a tree in an orchard.
On the tree is a gold apple
and in the apple are seeds
and in one of the seeds is the heart
of the great giant.

Or the giant has set his heart
in a gold ring.
You might mistake it for a red ruby,
but it is really his heart.

Or the giant has taken his heart out
and placed it in the body
of this beautiful lady.
See—she has two hearts.

It is foolish of the giant
to keep his heart out of his body
in ring or apple or lady,
in mine or well or cave

but heroes must always take advantage
of the foolishness of giants
and try not to be like them.

Once upon a distant time
when the gods rewarded good,
a mother and two daughters lived
in a farmhouse near a wood.

Small was the house, the fields were small,
with a small barn and a small stable,
some hens, a horse, a cow, that gave
the milk and butter for the table.

Now if the mother had been wise
they might have lived together well,
busy and happy all the year,
with food to eat and some to sell.

But she so favoured Gwendolyn,
her elder, stupid, lazy daughter,
Elsie, the younger, worked alone,
and milked the cows, and carried water.

Elsie was both good and gay,
kind to the poor, the old, the weak,
and beautiful as she was kind,
with golden hair and rosy cheek.

(No wonder Gwendolyn disliked her.
I fear I might have loathed her too
if I had a younger sister:
alas, dear Reader, so might you.)

From the wood a friendly witch
came to watch these sisters work,
saw how Elsie slaved all day,
how her sister used to shirk.

One day, then, the witch approached,
dressed in ancient skirt and veil,
sat beside the well where Elsie
came to fill her water pail.

"Prithee, girl," the witch demanded
(she had read an older tale)
"Give me water. I am weary
and my strength and courage fail."

Elsie gave her water then,
brought her bread and country cheese,
helped her find her pathway home,
chatted to her at her ease.

Homeward then she took her way
to the farmhouse where her mother
and her sister waited for her,
grumbling of her to each other.

"Why," the angry mother asked,
"Did you wander to the wood
while the chores were to be done?
I'll be bound you sought no good."

Elsie opened up her lips,
but from her mouth when she would speak
roses mixed with rubies fell,
the garden blossomed at her feet.

"Gwendolyn," the mother said,
"You too must seek to win your fortune.
Diamonds and wheat may be your gift
if fairies give you too a portion."

So Gwendolyn, that idle girl,
went grumbling off with swinging pail
and found again the ancient woman,
with ragged cloak and dusty veil.

"A gift, fair girl," the old witch said.
"Give me a drink of good well water.
I'm tired, I'm lost, my legs are sore:
help me, as you would help your mother."

33 "I have no time to waste on you,"
Gwendolyn said, the rude and greedy.
"I came in search of fairy gifts,
and not to help the old and needy."

The witch then flung aside her veil.
She was as grand as any queen,
and tall, and young, and proud, and straight,
she stood and stared down Gwendolyn.

"Girl," she said, "who would not give
to the poor and weak and old
even a single kindly word,
you too will suffer age and cold;

suffer from unkindness too,
bitter thoughts and bitter words.
If you have children they will cut
your heart to bits with swords."

Frightened, Gwendolyn rushed home,
screaming loudly as she ran,
and with every scream there fell
a toad or frog to ground.

Sad that toads and frogs should creep
where her sister's roses grow
and where Elsie's rubies lie
Gwendolyn's worms and spiders go.

Moral

Who speaks kind words speaks roses, say
white witches and good godmothers.
Now pity those like Gwendolyn
(or like your Author) who fare worse.

In real life
the kind and unkind sisters
are usually the same person.
Regan-Goneril and Cordelia
share bodies on alternate days,
scold their father and then weep over him.
They are forever poisoning each other
or putting each other into prison.

How can the old king know
when his favourite daughter
will escape from her wicked sister's eyes
and kneel before him?

Toads and roses fall together
from the cruel tender mouth
of the Kind-Unkind,
double gifts
of the godmother witch.

Stage setting

The great grey winged and feathered clouds
sweep over the prairie sky.
Thunder rolls in the distance.
A dog barks in the yard below.

Old Lear, the crazy king,
caught in a storm,
found only a hovel's roof
to keep him warm,
no palace for his bare bones.

Trust not to age or blood,
trust not to riches,
trust not to your body's children
that they will not be bitches
or arrant knaves.

But fools may help you some,
and storms will not deceive you,
and those with harshest tongue
may most relieve you
when you are most in need,
like Lear, the crazy king.

Fool's song

If chimney pots fall down
and the world is shaken,
what do cats and suns care
if they've no harm taken
when chimney pots fall down?

When cats lie in the sun
and suns lie in the sky,
if chimney pots are shaken
what care I?—
since cats lie in the sun.

Even Lear
was not too old to learn,
old Lear, the child again,
taught by his wicked daughters;
the fool Lear, taught by his fool;
tempestuous Lear, taught by the tempest;
royal Lear, taught by Poor Tom;
blind Lear, taught by a blind man.

And what did you learn,
when the rain came and your wits turned?
What did you learn, old man?
that the gods are just? or crazy?
that hearts can break at eighty
as well as at eighteen?
that the universe
is no flatterer?
Or did you learn chiefly
the meaning of the word "never"?

Whatever your learning,
it came too late for life.
Whatever your learning,
it could only be of use
as a warning in a tale,
as a halo over your white head
where you stand on the stage forever
holding your beloved dead
in your dying arms.

Selections from a longer poem

I PSYCHE AND THE LAMP

So, wearied in her mind with questionings,
Tossed between doubt and doubt, wishing to have
Some certain knowledge, be it evil or good,
And troubled even by the side of love,
She lay awake when he seemed fast asleep.
Her heavy eyes, unvisited by sleep,
Searched in the darkness, but could trace no features
In the face beside her, known but never seen.
She knew where the lamp was and where the matches,
And where the knife too that her sisters gave her,
Could find them in the dark; but in her mind
She hunted for them often, often lit
The lamp, often stood poised, the knife
Clasped in her frightened hand, before that hour,
Not able longer to bear doubt, she crept
Out from the bed, and softly tiptoeing,
Half hesitating, half turning back, and then
Stepping with resolution, reached the lamp,
And put her fingers round its glassy base.
And still, she thought, if the voice called out, "Psyche,
Where are you, Psyche?" such grace was in that voice
She would put down the lamp, turn back, and know
She knew his features by its music.

Her love was sleeping, though, and no voice spoke.
Here were the matches, waiting by the lamp,
With the knife near them, hidden in a drawer.
Now, when the lamp was lit, shading the flame
To keep from waking those still-drowsy eyes,
Back to the bed she tiptoed, knife in hand,
And bent above the pillow. There she paused
Awhile before she dared to look;
Then, bending down, she saw the handsome boy
Asleep and dreaming, with his head flung back,
One arm still resting in her empty place.
Joy and relief wheeled in her dizzy head.
The treacherous lamp shook in one trembling hand,
While from the other slipped the cruel knife
And woke and wounded love.

Now Psyche as a pilgrim wandered forth
To seek her love.
She must wear out seven pairs of iron shoes
And fill seven vials full of tears before
She found her love again. It was December,
A bitter day, with wind heaping the snow
Into great drifts, in which poor Psyche floundered,
For all the roads were blocked—no snow-ploughs then.
Yet she continued: she was used to snow,
No town-bred girl from the tropics. She'd survive.
So on she struggled, with spruce on either side
Loaded with snow, or sometimes past a farmhouse
With children out in front, playing at snowballs.
The wind died down, and the cold air stood still;
The snow stopped drifting, hardened into crust,
A smooth, hard surface over which she walked
With ease, held up even on iron shoes.

Under the blue, bright sky of the afternoon
The crust shone blue; but when night came it sparkled
Bright as the stars that sparkled over it,
Those small, hard lumps of ice that shine in the sky.
And as she travelled under the eye of the moon
She came in view of a great mountain height.
At first it looked of glass, but was cold ice,
Covered with sprinkled snow. Straight in her road
It lay, and she could see no path around it.
So sheer the ice was that she could not climb it.
She must go back and ask the nearest farmers—
A long way back they lived—another way,
Or give the whole trip up and go back home.

But as she sat in sorrow on the ground,
Bitterly chewing in her mind the crust
Of grief, her wandering eye caught sight
Of a great bird's skeleton, the bones plucked clean,
And "Oh," she thought, "if that bird were alive,
I'd sit on his back, and his great flapping wings
Would lift me past this mountain." Then some voice,
Perhaps the bird's own, whispered her to take
The bones of the skeleton and make a ladder,
And with this ladder climb across the mountain.
And she obeyed, and with laborious steps
Climbed up the mountain and down the other side.

A strange and dangerous place that mountain was,
With cliffs and crags of ice, and slopes of ice,
Shining all colours in the light of the moon;
Yet with her ladder she journeyed safe enough
Until she came to near the foot of it,
And then the bones gave out. "What shall I do?"
She thought. "It's still too far to jump."
But then she took the knife out of her pocket,
And cutting off her finger, used that bone
As the last rung of the ladder. Blood ran down
The icy slope, and from the snow there sprang
A rose or two, thinking that June had come.

III   ADVENTURE UNDERGROUND

So Psyche started once more on her travels.
She had not far to go to find the mouth
Of the underworld, for that lies always near,
Though guarded by an iron gate. She knocked
Awhile before the porter came, a man
Forbidding in his look, who opened up
The gate a crack, but did not let her in.
"What is your name?" he asked. "Love's wife, called Psyche,

Sent by my husband's mother for a box
     Someone's to give her." Then he let her in,
     Barring the gate behind her. "You may wish,"
     He said, "you had not come. The way is long
     And full of dangers. But that is your affair.
     There is the path you follow." This dark path
     Led through a twilight landscape, sloping downward,
     Where fog crept round her, and she could not see
     More than a step ahead at any time.
     So down the gradual, perilous descent,
     She felt her way, and stumbled
     Sometimes on stones half-hidden in the road,
     Or felt a bramble catching at her skirt.
     At a turn in the path, the fog decreased a little,
     But then she wished it back, for here she saw
     A pack of hungry bears that she must walk through.
     She stopped to get her courage up, and they
     Advanced to meet her, growling. Almost she
     Said farewell to her life, but then she thought
     Of her husband, and remembrance of his face
     Strengthened her to go on. They stood aside,
     Though with a hungry look at her, and she
     Went on her way beyond them. No life stirred
     For some time on the path. Only dead bracken
     Crackled beneath her feet. And then she heard
     A noise like steam escaping; wondering,
     She approached the noise, and sudden from the ground
     A thousand snakes' heads started. Round they coiled
     And darted out fierce tongues, wreathing their bodies
     In oily convolutions. These frightened her
     More than the bears; but them she also passed,
     While they upreared themselves to sting, but failed.
                              Beyond the snakes
     There was a narrow valley, piled with heaps
     Of slimy ordure, giving forth a stench
     That almost turned her stomach. Here she might
     Have died of suffocation, but pure air
     Breathed in upon her when she thought of love.

41   So down through varied dangers and strange scenes
She made her way, until at last she came
To the door of the dark central chamber, guarded
By all the foes she'd passed before, and more:
Fire-breathing lions, witches with red eyes
Like coals of fire, giants with flaming torches;
But through them all she made her way, and opened
The heavy door, that creaked to let her past.

Inside the dim-lit room, she looked around,
Expecting to find more and still more giants.
But nothing stirred within. The place was empty.
There was no furniture, only bare floors,
And dark, cavernous walls. Then she sat
Down on the damp, cold floor and waited there
Long hours, not knowing what to do,
And in the blankness almost she forgot
Her husband's face, and almost fell asleep.
But still she did not sleep, and finally
She felt a something moving in the room,
A breath of wind, perhaps; it came towards her,
And she half-glimpsed a figure draped in shadows
That bent above her, caught her by the hand,
And pressed within her palm a metal box,
Then vanished. Was the figure real? she wondered.
But the box was real enough. She felt
The carving on its cover. This must be
The box she should take back.
                    So now, arising,
She made her way back through the sentried door,
Back the long pathway through the snakes and bears,
Through the still-foggy landscape, to the place
Where the porter stood, surprised to see her living.
Yet he said nothing, but unbarred the gate
And let her through once more. And so she came
Up to fresh air and sunlight once again.

If Psyche had not found
Cupid above or underground;
if all the tasks she ever strove
to do won not his love;
if all the helpers proved untrue,
and angry Venus beat her black and blue;

I wonder then
if Psyche would have sought him still,
or turned to men
less godlike but of easier will?

But luckily
for Psyche and for Cupid too,
he did not try her strength to that degree,
but when she sought him
came to meet her: so
the poets say, and surely they should know.

Rosa

Often as Rosa was in love,
each time she thought it was forever,
for this one had enchanting eyes,
and that one was much more than clever;

and one she liked the way he kissed,
and one the way he never did,
one for Byronic melancholy,
and one for gaiety and wit;

one for his sturdy common sense
and one because he was a fool,
and one whose tantrums all were hot,
and one whose blood was always cool.

Each time she thought it was forever,
and every time her heart was broken,
and yet she woke another day
to see another love awaken.

Willie Lump Lump

The loneliest man in the world is dead
the newspaper says;
or maybe he was just
the ugliest man in Canada,
with a disease
which made tumors grow
at the nerve ends of his skin,
so that even in penitentiary
people called him Willie Lump Lump.

His family was ashamed of him;
waitresses wouldn't wait on him;
he had no job.
He tried to kill himself three times
but always failed.

But his one friend
a widowed old age pensioner said
"He was a very nice man.
He wanted to work as a night watchman
because of his face, you see."
But now he is dead.

Death is no plastic surgeon
but he does shape new faces
gradually.

In the Carleton Street graveyard
a fat woman in a fur coat
is feeding pigeons.
She is pulling scraps
from her shopping bag,
and dozens of pigeons
cluster on the snowy ground
or on a park bench
or on one of the tombstones.
One or two squirrels
are hopping towards
the congregation.

Catching sight of me,
she is embarrassed,
caught like a saint or a child
in absurd beneficence.
"Hurry," she calls
to the approaching squirrels.

Romance

Mary tells me she admires the salmon
because it is such a romantic fish.
It travels two thousand miles in order to spawn,
then dies in a ritual of love and death,
its flesh feeding new generations.

But I am relieved to discover
that only Pacific salmon
are in fact so feeble.
Atlantic salmon make the trip to spawn
several times,
though every spawning
leaves another scar
and they are ringed like trees.

HESTER PRYNNE

The great red A that frightened children so
burned on her breast. They thought that she was Sin.
Embroidered flame announced the flame within,
blazing on blackness that was deep as woe.

She was like forests that are dark as night,
haunted by witches and by savages,
where fruits and mosses cling to ancient trees
and men are lost and fade away from sight;

or like an ocean into which men fall
and drown themselves within the salty flood.
Over their heads there flowed her tidal swell,
the lunar promptings of her flesh and blood.

Dimmesdale was drowned. Old Roger, on the shore,
Envied his drowning. He could do no more.

ROGER CHILLINGWORTH

Revenge and love, twined in a single strand
like lovers' hair in our grandfathers' days,
wound round his heart and strangled it. His gaze
was like a lover's, which must understand
all motions, probe the depths of the loved eyes
for all past secrets and dead sympathies.

Stealthy and slow, his undiscovered lust
moved sidelong to unbutton Dimmesdale's mind.
He must possess his thoughts; his hands must find
his heart, and feel his agony undressed.

His victory was to know the man had sinned.
But in his conquest he himself was lost
and in his owning he himself was owned.
Dimmesdale possessed him, and the weak had won.

Pride of remorse devoured him day by day.
Not God could pardon, for his guilt was heaped
sky-high. Not tears, but blood, he wept,
poured out to God, his loving enemy.

The anguished copulation of a prayer
could not avail; for surely he had done
an evil act, was worse than others were,
since his unfaithfulness was to the One

and infinite God. This dark adultery
bred falsehood in the mind. It filled his heart
full of a strange and naked blasphemy,
and gave him dreams of terror. Waves of sweat

broke on him. He slept, and dreamed again
of Hester's flesh, that made and marred him man.

All's well that ends well

When Helen followed that ungrateful boy,
her husband, from one city to another,
schemed, wheedled, tricked, and used her honest craft
to get him and his ring—was he worth the bother?

How did she like her prize when she got home
with it to Rousillon? Was his curled hair
enough to make her happy, or did she long
for courts to visit and for kings to cure?

Did he flirt with other girls, find her pedantic,
her conversation too medicinal?
Did she freeze his buddies out of the castle gates
or retreat from them into her own still

feminine chamber? Did her mother-in-law
wrangle with her at times? When she was alone
was she sometimes glad Bertrand was out of sight?
And what was breakfast like at Rousillon?

III
INANNA

Who was the last person to say a prayer
to the old gods, to Jupiter or Diana,
Ceres or Venus? And did whoever said it
say it with belief, or only as a sort of charm
half remembered from childhood?
Did someone say to her (I know she was a woman)
"You mean you still believe
all those old stories? All the modern people
have changed over to the new religion.
Nobody in town,
nobody with any education,
would pray now to one of those dusty ancients.
It's not fashionable—
anyhow, it's not even legal."

But somewhere in the country
in a hovel under trees
some old crone dying in her bed
whispered a name she had heard in childhood
to protect her from the dark,
from the shades of the underworld;
and the goddess of hearth or orchard,
of moon or love or wisdom,
or the god of vine or thunder,
or the goatfoot god,
came and took her hand,
descended with her into the shadows,
and (except by the lips of lying poets)
was never called back again.

50   Could you still be called back,
      ancient gods and goddesses?
      Or have you slept so long
      with no cries from your children
      that there will never again be a morning for you?
      Deities with so few petitions
      might well be the most easily secured,
      the best listeners.

      Oh seaborn Venus, heavenly Juno,
      oh dark Persephone, daughter of the Earth,
      from where you rest in the arms of death
      I call you.

      Dionysus, true Vine,
      hand me your chaliced blood.

Lady, the unknown goddess,
we have prayed long enough only
to Yahweh the thunder god.

Now we should pray to you again
goddess of a thousand names and faces
Ceres Venus Demeter Isis
Inanna Queen of Heaven
or by whatever name
you would be known

you who sprang from the sea
who are present in the moisture of love
who live in the humming cells
of all life
who are rain
with its million soft fingers

and you who are earth
you with your beautiful ruined face
wrinkled by all
that your children have done to you

sunlike lady
crowned with the whirling planets.

Lady of peace, of good counsel,
of love, of wisdom

we invoke your name
which we no longer know

and pray to you
to restore our humanity
as we restore your divinity.

Was it not the goddess of the moon
who destroyed Actaeon in her forests?
He came too close to her, he gazed
without protection at her nakedness.

She turned him into a wild stag,
and his own hounds
his servants
leaped at his throat and killed him.

Was it not his fault,
the foolish man
who came into the moon's forests,
who climbed the moon's mountain,
who looked too close
at the naked moon?

Inanna

When the goddess Inanna
descends to the underworld

she must take off her crown
and go without pride

she must take off her jewels
and go without adornment

she must take off her clothes
and go without veils.

The queen of the sky
must sink into the ground;
the queen of the sunrise
must swallow darkness;
the queen of life
must remove her gown of flesh
and sleep in dust.

ANNUNCIATION

Annunciation comes in spring. The snow
is melted to puddles in the sudden sun.
Packs of it slide like thunder from barn roofs,
with icicles turned to water from the eaves.
Over the brown and muddy fields the crows
flap cawing, and the earliest song sparrow
sings love songs to the earth.

And now the Angel, walking through the yard,
moves Mary-ward; in this gray farmhouse
she may be in the kitchen kneading bread
or upstairs making beds, or in the dairy
churning the cream to butter; or she stands
here in the window where the sun pours love.

The earth waits
for the fall of the seed in its furrows,
for sun and rain.
Gently it will protect, with its veins nourish
grass, violets, oats,
the rich and foaming clover.
In time it will be
perpetual mother.
But now it is young and cold from the snow; it turns
awakening
towards the sun and the love song of the bird.

VISITATION

It was a summer day that Mary came
to see her cousin, old Elizabeth,
that woman who expected a strange birth,
whose spring had come in winter of her life.
She walked the dusty road into the village
between the hayfields ripening on each side
and all the richness of the summer's green.
She too was a field, she thought, a blossoming tree
whose fruit would ripen slowly in the winter.

54   Now there were children sitting in the pasture,
deep in the clover and the foaming daisies,
hugging the patch of shade beneath the elm trees,
picking wild strawberries, pulpy and red and sweet.
They called to each other
across a world of green.

Her cousin, watching from the kitchen window,
had seen her coming, and slamming the screen door,
walked out to meet her, moving heavily,
she was so near her time.

BIRTH

The child was born in winter. Deep December
had piled the snow halfway to the barn roof.
The cows and horses huddled in the stable,
warming each other with their friendly breaths.
Under the pines the snow was blue and crusty,
and the white fields stretched cold beneath the stars.

It was a frosty night for love to come
into the world; but love, conceived in spring,
ripened to fullness in the autumn weather,
is born at last in winter, burning son
in the cold stable of our battered hearts.

Man with gospel message
(*Verbal transcription*)

I

(*Lazarus*)

When I was young
(the man says)
I died once
for twenty minutes.

My eyes have never seen
so clear again.
I saw inside,
I saw even the springs
inside my mattress.

II

(*Bible*)

What is wrong,
he says,
is all the churches.
What is wrong
is the way they worship texts

so that there was this woman
who burned out her eye
so that it would not see evil

and this man
who cut his child's hand off
for stealing honey.

III

(*Ghosts*)

It is the spirits that do all the harm
(he says).
All the spirits from the past invade you.
There was this girl
a French-Canadian girl
who had her body taken over by the ghost
of a tubercular German immigrant
and found she could only speak German.

Now you can't altogether blame the ghost—
she wanted a life, too, see?—
but it was sure hard on the girl
not to be able to speak
either of the right languages.

IV

(*Chosen People*)

God speaks to me, too,
and I tell you
he always speaks in English.

Every morning
just before breakfast
he speaks.

I have decided the Anglo-Saxons
are the chosen people.

V

(*Call to Action*)

I tell you it only needs a few people
to take over any one of these churches,
United Church or whatever.

It only needs a few people
to take over the governments
of countries.

It only needs a few people
to overturn the world.

Jesus revolution hits Alberta
A Group of Found Poems
(from *The Way*, vol.3 no.2, July 1972)

I

Look
the "unexpected"
is happening again
A special highlight
coming to Calgary.
Spiritual stampede
at Immanuel Assembly
17th Ave & 1st St. S.W. Calgary
Meet the Minneapolis God Squad
July 9 - 16
26 dynamic youth
who "wowed" thousands
during recent Caribbean tour.

II

I FOUND HAPPINESS

I thank the Lord
for all He's done for me . . .
saved me at the age of eight . . .
at the age of 17,
I turned my back on Him
completely, ran wild,
hitchhiked all over the country . .
my problem was
I did not fear God. . . .

Then I came to the city of Red Deer
and my ideas about God changed.

I believe
that my testimony is typical. . . .

III

The camp you cannot afford to miss.
FAMILY CAMP Bible Conference.
Please bring all your bedding supplies
(a warm bed roll
or adequate sleeping bag,
pillow, blankets, bed sheets). . .
Girls: hot pants and mini skirts
are undesirable dress during camp.

IV

Our family
moved to Alberta in 1969
and I started going to university,
a place which is as close
to HELL on earth
as man has ever been.

V

JESUS T-SHIRTS
in medium and large sizes
are now available. . . .

The following messages
appear on shirt fronts:
1. God is Love
2. Jesus Loves You
3. Jesus is Lord
4. Praise the Lord
5. Turn from your sin
and believe the Good News of Jesus
or else. . . .

VI

Jesus is where it's at.
Jesus is coming!

Heaven is not necessarily true
because I would like to believe in it—
No, nor necessarily false either.
How do I know what is or is not,
when I don't even know what is this hand
that holds my blue pen
or what makes the pen blue?
It looks the way it does because of the way
it absorbs or throws off light
or the way light hits my eye,
whatever light is
or whatever my eye is.
The pen's solidity,
like its blueness,
is probably a kind of illusion.

All this time, all this year, spent
talking to students about books,
those solid three dimensional objects,
or reading the words of students
written with their blue pens

And I do not know, do not know,
cannot really tell them,
only know when I disagree with them,
do not know
what is poetry or what is blue
(though I look now at the sky
and see what is blue)
or if God and heaven are myths
(myth being a fancy literary name
for a lie).

60   I think I would like to turn my life
      back to page one and read it all again
      so maybe it would make sense
      because it seems I am still always
      asking the same questions
      that I asked myself (and sometimes answered)
      when I was ten or twenty,
      like Who am I?
      and Who are all these others?
      Whose novel is it
      that we have stumbled into?
      Does the author intend
      a happy ending or an endless fall
      down through light years of space?

      Why do I sometimes wake up
      during my dreams
      convinced the dream is true?

Playing Indian in the back orchard
with a feather stuck behind my ear
dropped from one of the moulting hens,
I believed in the existence of Indians
neither more nor less than I believed in Robin
     Goodfellow
or ghosts or elves.
They were invented, maybe,
by Longfellow or Fenimore Cooper;
on the other hand (like ghosts)
might really be true.

Once an Indian woman came to the door
selling woven baskets
and little bunches of mayflowers.
But the woman looked no different
from any of the neighbour women
with a good tan.
No feathers.

My mother put lemon juice on her face
after being in the sun,
or sometimes cucumber,
to make sure her skin stayed white.
"Why do you want to tan?" she said.
"It makes you look just like an Indian."

Indians, my mother said,
used to live in the woods,
but didn't any longer.
Robin Hood had lived in the woods too,
and so had the Nut Brown Maid.
Now there were only bears and squirrels.
Anyhow I was not to go to the woods.
People got lost there.

It was only in *Hiawatha*
that Indians prayed to the Manitou.
Now they were Christians
the same as everybody else.

If I were an ant crawling on a blade of grass,
I would be unaware of all those beings
planning to step on me
or to spray me with insecticide.

If I were a giant so large I was invisible,
I would step peacefully from planet to planet
and stride beyond all these troubles.

But I am just the wrong size. I am human.

IV
PILGRIM

It is always the youngest son or the fool
who accomplishes the adventure,
though he sets out after the others leave.
He is the one who finds the magic well
and brings back the water that will cure his father.
He picks the golden apple from the tree
guarded by the great green dragon.
He kills the giant, steals his moneybags,
and makes off with the giant's daughter
or the princess whom the giant had wickedly
        kidnapped.

His brothers always laugh at him to begin with,
say he is a child, a mother's pet,
or they plot against him, hide him in a well;
but in the end he has to rescue them,
free them from giants or famine,
share the moneybags, provide them with ladies
not quite so well-born as his princess
but good enough for them.

And it is always the youngest daughter or the ugly one
who is rescued or married by the hero,
changed from her dragon or frog shape by his kiss.
She is the one who makes a long journey
to find her husband or her missing brother,
who guides the hero through a maze of dangers
and when he is dead takes all his scattered bones
and sews them back together,
breathes life into them
so that he wakes again.

It is the youngest son or youngest daughter
who stops to pet the cat, talk to the bear,
share crumbs with birds,
help the lame old woman,
listen to the blind man
telling stories by the kitchen fire.

Are youngest children
really the most kind or the most adventurous?

Or is it the youngest son or the fool
who sings the songs?
Is it the youngest daughter or the ugly one
who tells the stories?

My unkind self

Why do I feel guilty towards the old woman
who lives next door,
who brings me date squares and fancy cakes
and wants to talk to me?

She asks me questions,
but is too deaf to hear
any of my answers.

I think she has invented a whole
life for me.
She has decided that I am a nurse,
married, but separated from my husband,
and she supposes that I have a daughter
living somewhere with my parents.
She is sorry for me,
and thinks I need to be fattened up,
though I tell her desperately that I am overweight,
and would like to tell her that I don't like cake.

Should I bake cookies just to take her some?
Should I ask her about her grandchildren?
(But she can't hear me.)

I am afraid my face shows
that I am not interested.
I am afraid that if she were a white witch
she would never be tempted to give me my three
        wishes.
If I were younger, I could pretend
that I would never live to be so old.

What magic caves and orchards
could have held more marvels
than the child's real world?
The black cat suckling her kittens
at small pink breasts;
the eggs, still warm from the cackling hen,
brought in from the straw-smelling henhouse;
ants in the barnyard,
marching in columns, carrying small bundles,
under the tall sunflowers;
the dust in a column of sunshine;
your own shadow, growing or diminishing.

Or even toys, a horseshoe-shaped magnet,
or the wooden blocks with which you built castles,
or the fat wooden man who stood up again
when you knocked him down,
or the inherited glass fire engine,
or the paper dolls cut from Eaton's catalogue,
or the swing under the trees
where you flung yourself at the sky.

And marvellously, as with a charm
(like the one you said rubbing your baby warts
with a cut potato),
they have all disappeared.

Paper dolls burned;
blocks, toys become rubbish;
the cat, hens, ants, sunflowers
long ago dead;
the dust reconstituted
to other dust.

Even the shadow the child cast
is not the same shadow.

Mirrors are always magical.
So the child knows
who first sees one: the strange object
in which the other little girl appears
wearing the same dress, encircled in the same arms;
smiles, frowns, looks puzzled, cries, all the same
but somehow different.
For the other child does not have flesh, feels shiny to
     touch
and cold like the mirror's surface.

Mirrors are magic, and behind their surface
surely there is another Alice world
where you can walk and talk.

Mirrors are solid lakes,
and you could drown
beneath them if their outer layer cracked,
spin down and meet your real self far below,
a mermaid princess combing out your hair
before a magic mirror.

Night air

"Come in, come in out of the night air," my aunt
     called.
"You shouldn't be outdoors in the night air."
And she summoned us in
from the sweet, dangerous, witching breath
of the evening-fragrant flowers.

Sweet, hot, and damp the air was.
We had played hopscotch in the liquid dusk.
I had just learned three new words:
twilight, honeysuckle, whippoorwill.
Now that night had come
there was no telling when it would be over.

Reading *As You Like It* reminds me
how I read it as a child, and thought
it could take place in the bush somewhere
beyond the cow pasture
where there were deer and chipmunks
and the fern-tasting blueberries grew.

But Orlando never came wandering
past with poems to stick on trees,
and I never saw Rosalind sitting
on the log fence of the pasture
making witty conversation
with melancholy Jaques.
There were no dukes eating picnic lunches,
or courtiers to sing to them,
and not even Touchstone
on a day's jaunt from the city
gingerly avoiding the
dried pats of cowdung.

But "What is poetical?" Audrey asked.
"Is it honest?"
                    Touchstone said no.

Meanwhile, while Troy was being besieged,
life went on in Ithaca as usual.
Penelope did her weaving.
Telemachus was growing up.

All through my childhood
Hitler goose-stepped on the front page,
Mussolini spoke to crowds from balconies.
My cousins and I made mudpies,
played "London Bridge is Falling Down,"
worried about other things
than Spain and Ethiopia.

I grew up. I went to classes
in a quiet town by a river
while London was being blitzed
and bombs dropped on Hamburg;
and what I remember about D-day
is having tea with lettuce sandwiches.

No doubt the day of Waterloo
there were births and marriages
as well as deaths.
No doubt on Judgment Day
there will be someone out selling hot dogs,
and children will cool themselves
with ice-cream cones.

Weep for Troy in flames
after all these centuries.
Again the palaces
slums and highrises
crumble with the heat.

Again we have carried
with our own hands
destruction into our city.

We shall become once more a story
mostly false
of heroes and beauty
praised by the blind.

Some day our city
will again be excavated
if there are any hands to excavate
these ashes, these broken dishes,
these heaps of
garbage, bones, used cars,
old tin cans, plastic,
this discarded
universe.

Disembarking from our aircraft at the city,
we were met by men and women dressed to kill
in sombreros, fancy waistcoats, and cowboy boots.
"Welcome," they cried heartily.
"Welcome to our city,
the Gateway to the Golden West."
They greeted us with badges and handshakes.
Some of them even embraced us,
while children handed us folders,
and a band played stridently
in the background.

We pushed our way through the packed airport
looking for someone who looked to be waiting for us,
but the man who was supposed to meet us
was not there,
and when one of us tried to telephone him
the operator said there was no such person.

We lugged our heavy bags
out to the sidewalk
and waited for our unknown taxi driver.

I kept intending to write a poem
about Alden Nowlan writing a poem
in the Winnipeg air terminal;
but he was always escaping,
flying off to a telephone booth,
zooming over the telegraph wires
            like Icarus
to some fantastic country,
while I was still sitting
in the Winnipeg air terminal
beside a potted palm
trying to draw a picture
of a heavy bearded man
            writing
with a ballpoint pen
in his little black notebook
            and stopping now and then
to draw funny pictures.

Reading a note about you,
I suddenly realize why you always seem familiar
when I see you at poetry readings.
Your birthday, I read, is December 30.
You share the same birthday with my father
and my eldest brother.
So I grew up with the voices of those Capricorns,
the long loping sentences, the easy gestures,
the anecdotes going on forever
with my non-talkative mother sometimes trying to
     halt them;
my brother drunk and singing all night
his parodies of Baptist hymns;
my father clowning
with some story about his days in the army
        ("So he says to me, Sarge . . .")
and suddenly in the midst of clowning sad,
sad to tears as my mother never was.

And I, not born under Capricorn,
never able to tell a funny story
all the way through
without breaking down somewhere in the middle,
I don't know you, mightn't like you if I did
(don't often write letters to my brother)
but nevertheless I play over a record of your poetry
to hear again what seems a family voice.

The witch is young.
Her uncoiled hair
slides down her back.
Her gaze is clear,

her forehead smooth,
her smile discreet,
her manner guarded,
distant-sweet.

The spirit who
obeys her spell
I think is tricky
Ariel.

She reads my palm
my horoscope.
I listen with
half-mocking hope,

but wonder
what her fate will be
who smiles and tells
my fate to me.

Almost I can see the room, almost:
the drawing room lit by one large gas lamp,
the chinese wall paper, the pianoforte,
the silver tea service,
a green Empire sofa by the wall.

The gentlemen have come from the dining room
not drunk but jovial
after their claret.
They talk well.
They sit with the ladies and sip bohea,
recovering from their argument about politics.

Sir Walter's wife wears red feathers
and too much rouge.
One pretty daughter, dressed in white,
is playing
the fashionable harp.
The other sings.

At ten exactly
(since they were up at dawn)
they will light tapers
and troop upstairs to bed.
It has been a pleasant evening
in a civilized city.

Most of the young people in the room
will die young;
but luckily
they imagine for themselves
a long life.

Will the ghost of the dead poet
be put off by all that scrubbing and polishing
the house has had since he lived in it?
Or by the crowds of the faithful
buying postcards and guidebooks?
A ghost, one imagines, likes things as they were.

Still, familiar objects have been gathered,
locks of hair, snuff boxes,
a knife and fork he used, wine glasses,
a family Bible, scraps of poems, love letters,
even an oatcake cooked by the poet's wife,
preserved under glass. These may bring him back.
Afer all, hasn't the race always saved
dishes and food for the dead?

And there are portraits, real and imaginary,
of the poet, his wife, children, mistresses.
He was more rugged, more like a farmer,
than the portraits showed, they say.
And his eyes glowed, the young boy remembered
who spoke to him only once.
There were never such eyes
in any other man's head.

Ghost, ghost, you are more alive still
than half the people in this room.

This is the true land of fairy tales,
this countryside of sullen beauty
heavy beneath dark trees. The brown smell of wood
lingers about it. Sawdust penetrates
every corner. You smell it, mixed with manure,
in the restaurant with its moosehead, or, like dim must,
in the little movie house.

The short street swims in dust and sunshine, slides
into a country road, and crosses the bridge
across the log-filled river where men walk,
balancing on the logs, and a single rowboat
holds a group of boys, their dark, round heads
bent close together. Sunshine, wind, and water
carry together the floating smell of boards.

Across the bridge is pasture; later, woods.
This is a land
not settled yet by its generations of settlers.
Wildness still lingers, and the unfriendly trees
suffer, but do not shelter, man, their neighbour.
No Eden this, with parks and friendly beasts,
though hopeful settlers, not far distant, called
their country Canaan, New Jerusalem,
or even Beulah. Yet beauty here is solemn,
with the freshness of some strange and morning world.

At the last house on the edge of the woods, two
        children
sit on their swings, reading aloud to each other
a fairy tale of children in a wood.
Their mother, hanging up her Monday wash,
stops for a minute and watches flying over
the shining crows flapping their heavy wings.

My small, clean room has pink wallpaper.
The bed is high and white.
On a ledge above the window
are six books
and a model of a sailing ship.

In the backyard
one hen wanders through grass
among dandelions.
Another scratches in the brown earth
with one leg,
bending her head for worms.
A dog barks in the distance.

Beyond the green picket fence
there is a road,
but not many cars travel it.

Immigrants

There are swans on the pond
instead of the ducks which once swam there.
Brought to the town by airplane
they are not native, winter with difficulty,
are superior fragile birds.

I admire
their white graceful throats,
their easy motions,
but somehow liked the ducks better.

I grow too old for love—
have never cared for money—
and fame is youth's delusion,
who read Catullus
and wanted to save, like him,
some one thing—a sparrow, maybe—
from the cold touch of time

a small brown quivering bird
frightened
or a day, night, pair of hands
with veins running blue and prominent,
or a mole on the neck, moved in and out with breath.

I wanted to save breath
hold it caught in,
not released
until sometime centuries later
I might breathe it out
blow the hair of
someone sitting reading
not expecting a ghost.

But I thought then
there would always be books,
there would be
lamps or candlelight,
there would always be people
reading at night,
lonely, stirring up the fire,
inviting the spirits of the dead

to tell them about sparrows
or the veins in hands
or the feel of a ballpoint pen
grasped in dead fingers.

But how can there be poems
if there are no sparrows
and no people?
How can a ghost haunt
a world without houses?

Sometimes there are earthquakes in the mind.
It cracks and heaves
shakes off its top layers
and shows below
metals, fire, granite,
rivers flowing in a changed direction.

And there are buried cities
revealed again
streets and houses
completely furnished
the dead in agonized poses
petrified
or locked in love's embrace.

There is a child's doll with a broken head
there is a round striped ball
there is a broom made of branches
a picnic basket lying abandoned
under a tree

some faded flags and uniforms
discoloured
war posters.

One friend has killed himself; another dies
gradually operation by operation.
I too am breakable.
My flesh and bones have been renewed seven times
and yet they feel past scars and sprains.

Underground the mind is dark soil.
Through its cracks and crannies
silence seeps like rain.
Some time, after all that drought and hail,
the mind will be prairie in a good year,
will ripple wheat and lupines.

But what of the flesh, I ask?
What of the dead man's wounds?
What of your cancer-ridden cells?

What field of grain and poppies
can take the place of any pair of hands,
of the web of skin
covering bone, joint, and tendon?
Whose eyes will have
precisely the same colour in the iris?

But why do I grieve,
dying while I grieve?
The pattern of my atoms too will break.
Beyond the Milky Way
how many galaxies explode in light?

On the death by burning of
Kimberly Hammer, May 1972

Only the grandmother weeps—
the mother smiles, tearless,
the father also,
though panic clouds his eyes,
an effort
not to see.

A neighbour remembers
the child Kimberly
out walking at Christmas
wrapped for winter,
cheeks pink, eyes bright as candles,
saying,
"I like to walk in the cold. I like the cold."

When fire blazed through the tent,
when there was no cold,
did your young eyes see
all past and future blazing at once?

Knowing you will miss
our gradual years
the slow burn
of time in your flesh,
we are not sure
if what we feel is pity
or is envy.

Later, at night,
I awake cold in bed,
pile on winter blankets,
make a tent
of skin and blankets.

I sleep again, and dream
of you, Kimberly,
no child of mine, no relative,
a May candle
burning
in the dark.

The world is falling down.
Rocks crack and lava flows.
Trees break off from their banks,
are whirled down streams of flame.

Oh, where can I escape?

The voices of the dead
cry in the wind:
"Eden is buried,
there can be no return."

The voices of the unborn
never to be born
weep their betrayal:
there is no new heaven;
there will be no more sea.

Waiting room

My father stands in front of me
as we ride upstairs on an escalator.

Upstairs a small girl and an old woman
chant together, Time Time Time Time.

I sit down beside the child.
We are both waiting
for someone on the other side of the closed door.

Through an open window
we see green trees in an orchard.

Night is falling.
My father is somewhere else.

Lost

I dream I am honeymooning with my father
in a strange city.
Somebody says the word "incest"
and I run away.

I cannot find my way
in all these labyrinths.
There are miles of empty shop windows.
My feet are bleeding.
I carry my shoes in my hands.

I am not sure
if I am escaping from my father
or trying to find him again.

The girl and the man in the dream
wear animal skins, are hunters,
camp all night in a shack
in the wilderness.

It is a northern landscape
rugged.
The trees grow low
but hardy.

Ghosts come, ghosts of Indian warriors,
and encircle the camp.
There are strange wizard spirits
hobgoblins
dangerous
with candle eyes.

Nevertheless,
the man and the girl will survive,
are protected from ghosts

because—

There is some magic reason
but the dream did not reveal it.

I am of puritan and loyalist ancestry
and of middle-class tastes.
My father never swore in front of ladies,
as he always quaintly called women.
My mother thought that a man was no gentleman
if he smoked a cigar without asking her permission;
and she thought all men should be gentlemen,
even though a gentleman would not call himself one,
and all women should be ladies,
even though a lady would not call herself one.

I have never taken any drug
stronger than aspirin.
I have never been more than slightly drunk.
I think there are worse vices
than hypocrisy or gentility
or even than voting Conservative.

If I wanted to be fucked
I should probably choose a different word.
(Anyhow, I am not quite sure
whether it is a transitive or an intransitive verb,
because it was never given to me to parse.)

Usually I can parse words, analyse sentences,
spell, punctuate,
and recognize the more common metrical forms.

It is almost impossible
that I shall ever be
a truly established poet.

I shall visit the Holy Land
(the child said)
I shall carry a blue pitcher
on my head

I shall be Rebekah
at the well
I shall wear gold bracelets
and they will jangle

I shall be the Shulamite
I shall be Egypt's daughter
I shall marry Solomon
and die and live thereafter

I shall be the lady
who lived with seven men
she who gave water to the stranger
and was comforted again

I shall live in the old time
before I was born
and I shall turn again
turn and return